THERAPY

A Play By

Lonetta Thompson

THERAPY

A Play By

Lonetta Thompson

The Play Right Series

THERAPY
Copyright 2023 by Lonetta Thompson

All rights reserved. Printed in the United States of America. No parts of this publication may be reproduced in any manner without written permission except in the case of brief quotations embodied in critical analyses and reviews.

Library of Congress Number:

ISBN: 978-1-942081-36-4
A publication of The Jasper Project
Chapin, South Carolina

The Play Right Series

JasperProject.org

The Play Right Series

The purpose of the Jasper Project's Play Right Series is to:

Empower and enlighten audiences by allowing them insider views of the processes of creating theatre art;

Increase opportunities for theatre artists to create and participate in new art without the necessity of being attached to an existing theatre organization; and to

Provide more affordable and experimental theatre arts experiences for new and emerging theatre artists and their audiences; thereby expanding cultural literacy and theatre arts appreciation in the South Carolina Midlands.

FOREWORD

Three therapy jokes:

Number one: Patient says, "I don't know how to explain it. I'm just not sure about anything in my life." Therapist says, "And how does that make you feel?" Patient says, "…Well, I really don't know."

Number two: Patient says, "I don't think anyone really understands me." Therapist says, "what do you mean?"

Number three: Patient says, "I'm absolutely terrified of random letters of the alphabet." Therapist says, "Oh you are?" The patient screams. Therapist says, "I see, I see." The patient screams.

I stole those from the internet, of course. There are thousands of therapy jokes there. The topic fascinates. In less than ten seconds, I found over fifty movies about psychotherapy. A popular favorite, apparently, is *I Never Promised You A Rose Garden*, based on an autobiographical novel by Joann Greenberg, about a teenaged girl hospitalized with schizophrenic delusions that caused her to harm herself. My personal favorite is *Equus*, Peter Shaffer's exploration, based on a true story, into the mind of a boy who stabbed out the eyes of six horses—and how that exploration damages his psychiatrist.

We are drawn to such stories because we know that, deep down, they're about us, our secret, broken selves. They offer ways to peel the onion of our psyche and maybe find what's down there at the deep dark core. And apparently, we need such stories more than ever.

Consider these numbers: last year, the American Psychological Association reported that more than 41 million American adults received counseling and/or took medication for anxiety, depression or related illnesses. That's one in six of us. Mental Health America reports that a third of adults experiencing mental illness cannot gain access to treatment, because for every 350 adults, there is only one licensed mental health provider. Of those providers, 84% say they have seen a marked increase in referrals in the past several years, and 40% report being unable to meet that demand. Half say they are burning out. Pandemic, right?

Well, sure, but between 1999 and 2017—before the pandemic—the suicide rate increased by 33%. These are all reasons that Dr. Arthur C. Evans, the CEO of the APA, says we are in the midst of "a mental health tsunami."

There. Now you are ready to begin reading Lonetta Thompson's play *Therapy*, the winner of the Jasper Project's 2023 Play Right Series, which was created several years ago to connect theater creators with community producers and to support the state's playwrights. *Therapy* is, as you may have surmised, about the culture of psychotherapy we live in, and the good it does, and the harm it does, and to whom.

The Play Right Series started in 2017, when Randall David Cook's *Sharks and Other Lovers* was selected as the winner and, after its PRS debut, went on to full production at Greenville's Center Stage. It's a play about five people grappling with depression and fears of mortality. The series continued in 2022 with Colby Quick's *Moon Swallower*, a hilarious and oddly poignant play about a werewolf who webcasts out of his mother's basement, except maybe he's not a werewolf. Maybe he's just a really nice, wounded guy dealing with issues he thinks make him a monster. Maybe *every* good play is about psychotherapy, about people trying to peel their own onions. Maybe we hope they can help us not drown in the tsunami.

So enjoy Lonetta Thompson's play, *Therapy*, but be careful. It only *looks* like a comedy. At heart it's actually a subversive inquiry into the questions we ask ourselves about the comfort we seek.

Final therapist joke: How many psychologists does it take to change a light bulb? Only one, but there's a ten-month waiting list. Meanwhile, here's a leaflet about how to cope with despair.

Jon Tuttle
August 2023

PREFACE

This play had been part of my *Half-finished Projects Collection* for well over ten years before I dusted it off to submit it for the Jasper Project 2023 Play Right Series. I've always loved writing and can remember lying on my bedroom floor writing my first mystery (it was a short story) while watching The Cosby Show. And then there was the "what I did for summer vacation" story that included a ski cabin in the Swiss Alps, a grizzly bear and a ski instructor named Hanz (or was it Franz?) that saved my life. I don't think my teacher believed me, but the story got an A.

Anyway, somewhere along the line, I decided to focus more on acting than writing. (What can I say? I was hooked after playing Dorothy in *The Wizard of Oz* in the 5th grade.) And while I've had a lot of fun playing some amazing characters, I never stopped adding to my collection. I just couldn't finish anything!

And then came the Jasper Project Play Right Series and a gentle nudge from a friend. *Therapy* wasn't the script I intended to submit, but sometimes things just work out....

As someone who grew up in a world where therapy was taboo, I played around with counseling for years—never quite taking it as seriously as perhaps I should have. At some point, when trying to come up with ideas for a script, I wondered what my therapists (and there had been a few) must have thought of me. *Did they hate to see my name on their schedule? Was I a source of entertainment – the easy hour in their day? Were they happy (or worried) when I stopped coming?*

Conceived as a two-act play, my original idea was to write a play that - depending on how it was cast, would tell different stories, and elicit different reactions from audiences. Hence, the gender-neutral character names. I didn't want to define anyone, just tell what I thought was a universal story that everyone could relate to. Over the years as I continued to nitpick over what I'd written without really writing anything new, I started to question this idea—it was either really great or simply ridiculous. I don't know which one it was, but I decided not to follow through with it.

I realized I needed a connection to the characters I was creating, and I could only form that connection if I defined them. I felt like I was doing them a disservice by being ambiguous. That idea may have been intriguing conceptually, but the focus wasn't on the characters or their story – it was on the idea. I needed to "see" Dr. V and her patients and be able to identify with each of them on some level in order to make them real people. It was also the only way I could allow them to speak to me. I mean, I had to know who I was talking to.

I didn't set out to make any specific commentary on therapy or the professionals who provide it; I just wanted to put it and them on display in a way that was light and fun and interesting and hopefully, thought provoking. I do, however, wonder what my therapist would think of *Therapy*....

On that note, I'd like to thank all the mental health professionals who do this day in and day out. Bless you. And thank you Grae, Taylor, Elizabeth, and Carol – you are my inspiration.

And to each of you reading this, I hope you get a kick out of *Therapy*!

Lonetta Thompson
August 2023

Therapy was developed in conjunction with The Jasper Project's Play Right Series during the spring and summer, 2023, and received a public, staged reading at the Columbia Music Festival Association on August 6, 2023. Series judges were Sharn Hopkins, Darion McCloud, and Brooke Mogy Watkins. Community Producers and Play Right Series Sponsors were Anonymous, Cindi Boiter, Libby Campbell-Turner and guests, Shannon and Steven Huffman, Jack McKenzie, Betsy Newman, Bill Schmidt, Wade Sellers, Amy and Vincent Sheheen, Kirkland and James Smith, and Keith Tolen

Therapy was directed by Elena Martinez-Vida.
Cast and crew were as follows:

Dr. V	**Marilyn Matheus**
Alex	**Allison Allgood**
Max	**Michelle Jacobs**
Chris	**Richard Edward III**
Stage Manager	**Emily Deck Harrill**

SETTING

Traditional therapist's office – desk, bookcase, couch, armchairs, etc. Doors lead to the outer receptionist area and private bathroom.

CHARACTERS

Dr. V Mid/late 40s. Psychologist. Sincere.

Alex Mid 20s. Dr. V's outspoken niece.

Max Late 20s to mid-30s. Accidental professional, cavalier.

Chris Late 20s. High strung, generally uncomfortable.

THERAPY

A Play By

Lonetta Thompson

SCENE I

At rise: Alex is seated at the desk in the outer office. Max is sprawled out on the couch in the doctor's office. Toilet flushes. Dr. V enters drying hands, pauses and looks at her patient; her exasperation is obvious. She checks her desk phone and then cell, clearly frustrated by the lack of messages. Sits without speaking. She makes a point of checking the time, picks up her notebook and pen and clears her throat...

Initially, dialogue should move at a quick but not hurried pace.

DR. V.

    Okay, Max-

MAX.

    (Abruptly) I don't think I can go through with this.

DR. V.

    Why not?

MAX.

    Because.

DR. V.

    Because why?

MAX.

    Because I can't.

DR. V.

    Why can't you?

MAX.

    Because it's a waste of time.

DR. V.

What is a waste of time?

MAX.

This.

DR. V.

What?

MAX.

This.

DR. V.

What is this?

MAX.

Counseling. Head-shrinking. "Therapy."

DR. V.

Hmm. Is that what you think this is?

MAX.

Isn't it?

DR. V.

I don't know.

MAX.

You don't know! You don't know what you do?

DR. V.

Yes, I know what I do.

MAX.

Oh really? Then you know that this is a waste of time.

DR. V.

Actually, no I don't know that because what I do is not a waste of time.

MAX.

The hell it isn't. This is a waste of time and money.

DR. V.

I still don't know what this is.

MAX.

I'm leaving.

(She does not move.)

DR. V.

Why?

MAX.

Why what?

DR. V.

Why are you "leaving"?

MAX.

Because this is a waste of time, and I have better things to do.

DR. V.

Like what?

MAX.

Huh?

DR. V.

What better things do you have to do?

MAX.

I don't know. Anything is better than this.

DR. V.

Really?

MAX.

Yes, really.

DR. V.

(Closing notebook dramatically) Okay.

MAX.

Okay, what.

DR. V.

Okay, go do your better things. I certainly don't want to be the cause of your wasted time. My time, however, is quite valuable. I rarely waste it.

MAX.

You damn sure charge a lot for it.

DR. V.

Max - why must we go through this? You come in here at least twice a month, say a whole lot of stuff that amounts to absolutely nothing for fifty minutes, pay the $125 and schedule another appointment.

MAX.

Yeah. So?

DR. V.

So what the hell is wrong with you?

MAX.

I don't know. That's what you're supposed to be telling me.

DR. V.

You can't be serious.

MAX.

You say that every week?

DR. V.

I don't like you.

MAX.

What?! You can't say that to one of your patients.

DR. V.

But it's the truth. And counseling, head-shrinking, "therapy"— whatever you want to call this— is all about getting to the truth. My truth at this moment—is that I don't like you.

MAX.

So, now what?

DR. V.

So, now you leave.

MAX.

Really?

DR. V.

Yes, really.

MAX.

(Checking watch) But I still have time left.

DR. V.

So?

MAX.

So... I'm not going to just waste thirty minutes. That's like— 75 bucks. Do you know what I could do with 75 bucks? Shoot, I catch that Macy's shoe sale on the right day—

DR. V.

Max! What the hell is wrong with you?

MAX.

I don't know!

DR. V.

Then why don't you just tell me why you choose to come here and spend hundreds of dollars a month instead of going to the Macy's sale. I mean, seriously—they have one every week. Why come here and waste my time?

MAX.

Ah ha! I thought you didn't waste your time!

DR. V.

(Sighing) I don't waste my time. You waste my time, and you pay me to do it. Why?

MAX.

Because.

DR. V.

Because why?

MAX.

Because I need someone to talk to.

DR. V.

That does not explain why you come here. You have yet to talk to me.

MAX.

I'm trying.

DR. V.

No, you're not.

MAX.

Yes, I am.

DR. V.

No, you are not.

MAX.

YES. I. AM!

DR. V.

I don't like you.

MAX.

Stop saying that.

DR. V.

Tell me what's wrong.

MAX.

Nothing.

DR. V.

Then leave.

MAX.

No.

DR. V.

Why?

MAX.

Why what?

DR. V.

Why won't you leave?

MAX.

I will when my time's up.

DR. V.

You have no idea how close you are to your time being up.

MAX.

What does that mean?

DR. V.

It means I want to kill you.

MAX.

What the hell? I really don't think it's ethical for you to threaten one of your patients.

DR. V.

I didn't threaten you.

MAX.

Yes, you did! You just said you wanted to kill me.

DR. V.

I do. It's the truth.

MAX.

That's a threat.

DR. V.

No. It's not. I'm *going* to kill you is a threat. I *want* to kill you is the truth.

MAX.

But you said I was close to my time being up.

DR. V.

You are. *(Checking her watch)* Twenty-five minutes and your time is up.

MAX.

That's not what you meant.

DR. V.

It's not?

MAX.

No, it's not.

DR. V.

But it is what I said....

MAX.

Yeah....

DR. V.

So what the hell is wrong with you? Why are you here?

MAX.

I need help.

(Dr. V responds with a "no shit" look.)

...I don't know what to do.

DR. V.

About what?

MAX.

About my life.

DR. V.

What's wrong with your life?

MAX.

I DON'T KNOW. All I know is that something is wrong and I'm paying you $125 a week to figure it out. *(Silence...)* Helloooooo....

DR. V.

Get. Out.

MAX.

What?

DR. V.

Get out. Leave. Be gone. You...are hopeless. I can't help you. I swear to God Jesus Christ the Lord Almighty could not help you. Just go.

MAX.

But I don't want to go. And you really shouldn't be swearing to God. That's just wrong.

DR. V.

(Fed up) Maxine Elizabeth James- tell me what the hell is wrong with you or so help me, I am going to go from wanting to kill you to "sorry judge, but I just couldn't take it anymore" with the quickness.

MAX.

"With the quickness"?! Wow. Did you really just say that? I haven't heard that expression in years. And did you really just use my whole government name?

DR. V.

MAXINE!

MAX.

Okay. Okay. I'll tell you. But you may want to see someone about your anger issues. That can't be healthy.

(Beat. When she finally speaks, we don't know if her statement is true or just something she is saying to appease the doctor)

...I hate my job.

DR. V.

So, quit.

MAX.

I can't quit.

DR. V.

Why not?

MAX.

Because.

DR. V.

Don't start.

MAX.

Fine. Okay. I can't quit because...

DR. V.

Because?

MAX.

Because of the people I work with.

DR. V.

And?

MAX.

And what?

DR. V.

And what do the people you work with have to do with you quitting your job?

MAX.

Forget it. You wouldn't understand.

DR. V.

Yes, of course. Let's just forget it. I mean, why would I understand. As a psychologist who is trained to listen and understand and more importantly help you understand, why would I understand?

MAX.

You got jokes.

DR. V.

No, Max. I do not got jokes. I most certainly do not got jokes. But hey, let's talk about jokes, shall we...

MAX.

Um. Okay. Have you heard the one about the crazy therapist?

DR. V.

No, I don't think I have. Let's hear it....

MAX.

I was kidding.

DR. V.

About what?

MAX.

About the joke.

DR. V.

Really?

MAX.

Yes.

DR. V.

So, there's no joke about a crazy therapist?

MAX.

I don't know. Maybe....

DR. V.

But you know a crazy therapist and her patient?

MAX.

Huh?

DR. V.

I am a therapist, Max. Specifically, a Doctor of Psychology. You were trying to call me crazy without actually calling me crazy. That's why you couched the remark in a 'joke', no?

MAX.

Huh?

(Awkward silence. Dr. V is writing in a notebook. Max is clearly uncomfortable. After a beat, the doctor looks up from her notebook.)

DR. V.

A man was walking down the street one day when he was brutally beaten and robbed. As he lay unconscious and bleeding, a psychologist, who happened to be passing by, rushed over to him and exclaimed, "My God! Whoever did this really needs help!"

MAX.

That's not funny.

DR. V.

Of course it is.

MAX.

No, it's not.

DR. V.

It is to me.

MAX.

Well, it's not to me.

DR. V.

Why?

MAX.

Why what?

DR. V.

Why wasn't it funny?

MAX.

It just wasn't.

DR. V.

Why?

MAX.

Because what's funny about someone getting beaten and robbed?

DR. V.

It's a joke.

MAX.

Well, it's not a funny joke.

DR. V.

Hm. *(Writes something in notebook.)* Okay. So, what do the people you work with have to do with whether or not you quit your job?

MAX.

What?

DR. V.

I was asking you about the people you work with.

MAX.

I know, but... the joke....

DR. V.

What about it?

MAX.

Um. Okay...nothing. Never mind. Uh, what was the question, again?

DR. V.

What do the people you work with have to do with whether you quit your job?

MAX.

It's not the people I *work* with; it's the people I work *with*.

DR. V.

Oh. *(Beat)* What?

MAX.

If I quit my job, everyone will think it's because of the people I work *with*.

DR. V.

Who?

MAX.

Who what?

DR. V.

(Deep sigh) You said you can't quit your job because everyone will think it's because of the people you work *with*...

MAX.

Right.

DR. V.

(Slowly...) Who is "everyone"? And who are the people you work "with"?

MAX.

(Slowly, mimicking Dr. V) "Everyone" is "everyone" and the people I work "with" is—*(dismissive)*—them.

DR. V.

Them? Hm. Interesting choice of words.

MAX.

What?

DR. V.

Again, who is everyone?

MAX.

I don't know. Family. Friends. Society. Everyone.

DR. V.

Society? Really? You think society is going to have a problem with you if you quit your job? Hm.

MAX.

Um, if you haven't noticed, society has a problem with everything.

DR. V.

Hm. *(Writes something in notebook.)* Interesting. And so, who is them?

(Silence...)

DR. V.

Max.

MAX.

Come on, doc. You know who "them" is.

DR. V.

How would I know?

MAX.

Because you know where I work.

DR. V.

And you know that's not how this works. Who is "them," Max? Stop bullshitting.

MAX.

Fine. "Them" is—the people I work with.

DR. V.

Damn it, Max - you know what? Screw it. By them, do you mean your co-workers?

MAX.

No. Well, yes. Some of them. Janet. I do hate Janet. Always trying to tell me how to do my job—

DR. V.

Max.

MAX.

Yes.

DR. V.

I really don't like you.

MAX.

(A beat) Yeah, well. I ain't that crazy about me either.

(Dr. V closes her notebook and stares at Max, hoping this is the breakthrough moment she's been working towards.)

DR. V.

What do you mean?

MAX.

Nothing.

DR. V.

Max. Don't start this again. You just said—

MAX.

I know what I said. Can we just get back to my crappy ass job, please?

DR. V.

Fine. Whatever you want, Max. Let's talk about your job and the people you work with. Wait—or is it the people you *work* "with"?

MAX.

See! That's why I can't quit. No one understands.

DR. V.

Understands what, Max?

(Max does not immediately respond. She gets up and starts pacing.)

DR. V.

Max, I can't help you if you don't tell me—

MAX.

Okay, fine. *(Beat)* No one understands what it's like to be surrounded all day by kids that, ugh, need stuff.

DR. V.

Stuff like what?

MAX.

I don't know—food, water, clothes. They make me sick.

DR. V.

Really?

MAX.

Yes. Really.

(Dr. V watches Max as she continues to pace. She takes a few notes before asking:)

DR. V.

Is that your truth?

MAX.

I guess it is.

DR. V.

Embrace it.

MAX.

What?

DR. V.

Embrace it. Embrace your truth.

MAX.

I don't understand.

DR. V.

What don't you understand?

MAX.

How I'm supposed to embrace hating kids!

DR. V.

Forget the kids. Embrace the hate.

MAX.

This is why I don't talk to you. What the hell does "embrace the hate" mean?

DR. V.

It means focus on the feeling, not the kids.

MAX.

What the hell does that mean?!

DR. V.

Ok. Listen carefully. You said you hate your job because you hate the kids because they need stuff, right?

MAX.

Yeah....

DR. V.

All I'm saying is forget about the kids. It's all about the feeling. Focus on how you feel and embrace it. Own it. Accept it. Don't fight it.

MAX.

At the risk of sounding like a broken record—what??

DR. V.

Own the feeling. Then and only then will you begin to understand it.

MAX.

What's to understand? I hate those kids.

DR. V.

No, you don't.

MAX.

Yes, I do.

DR. V.

No. You do not.

MAX.

YES. I. DO!

DR. V.

I promise you, Max. You do not hate the kids. You may hate that they need stuff—you may even hate that you're in the position of having to provide it—but you do not hate the actual children. If you did, you would not work at a group home for kids.

MAX.

That's just it. I never wanted to work there. I just needed a job.

DR. V.

You've been there ten years.

MAX.

Yeah, so.

DR. V.

Wow. *(Getting up heading to the door)* Look at the time.

MAX.

But—

DR. V.

Max, trust me. That's what you pay me for, isn't it?

MAX.

Are you sure?

DR. V.

Yes.

MAX.

Really?

DR. V.

Yes. Really.

MAX.

But how—

(Lights fade. End scene.)

SCENE II

Lights come up in outer office. Alex is seated at the desk reading a trashy novel. Chris enters and sits, unacknowledged by Alex. The desk phone rings, Alex does not answer. Her cell phones rings; she looks at it but does not answer. Chris is visibly upset. He fidgets, clears his throat, etc., to get Alex's attention. Max and Dr. V are still in the midst of their conversation in silence.

ALEX.

Oh, hey Chris. I didn't see you come in. *(Noticing his agitation)* What's wrong with you? Not enough raisins – or was it bran- in your Raisin Bran again?

CHRIS.

Excuse me?

ALEX.

I was just asking if you're okay?

CHRIS.

Yes, I'm fine.

ALEX.

You sure?

CHRIS

Yes, I'm sure.

ALEX.

You sure you sure?

CHRIS.

Yes.

ALEX.

Then why are you here?

CHRIS.

Excuse me?

ALEX.

I'm just saying—you look terrible. Seriously. I mean, even though technically I'm on my break, you know, I'm just saying...can I get you something? Water? Coffee? Cyanide?

CHRIS.

No, no. I'm fine! Did you say cyanide?

ALEX.

Okay, well. You just let me know if you change your mind.

CHRIS.

Ok. Thank you?

(Max enters from the doctor's office. She leaves without acknowledging Alex or Chris. Alex's cell phone rings just as Dr. V enters. Chris looks stricken.)

DR. V.

Chris, please wait for me in my office.

(Chris exits, giving Alex a pained look.)

DR. V.

...Were you torturing my patients, again?

ALEX.

Whatever. What took you so long? That's the third time this week I've had to deal with some crazy because a session ran long—

DR. V.

Did Mrs. Smith call?

ALEX.

Nope.

DR. V.

It's been a month.

ALEX.

Maybe you fixed her.

DR. V.

Unlikely. And I don't "fix" people.

ALEX.

This is true, but don't give up. I'm sure you'll get one right sooner or later.

DR. V.

(Turning into office) I could kill my brother for making me hire you.

ALEX.

He's already dead.

DR. V.

(Slams door, then to Chris) So sorry to make you wait. How are you?

(Unlike Max, Chris sits stiffly on the couch, clearly uncomfortable.)

CHRIS.

    Not so good, Dr. V. This has been just the absolute worst week of my life. I don't know how I made it through.

DR. V.

    Why don't you tell me what happened.

CHRIS.

    I don't know if I can. It's too painful to relive.

DR. V.

    Really?

CHRIS.

    Yes. Really!

DR. V.

    I can't help you if I don't know what happened.

CHRIS.

    It's the ringing! I can't stand the ringing!

DR. V.

    The ringing?

CHRIS.

    Yes! All the phones!

DR. V.

    Don't you work in a call center?

CHRIS.

The phones at work don't ring – they beep. It's the ringing I can't stand…

DR. V.

So…what ringing are you referring to, exactly?

CHRIS.

All the cell phones!

DR. V.

What?

CHRIS.

I can't stand all the cell phones. They're everywhere and they ring, and they ring, and they ring, ring, ring

DR. V.

I thought we worked through the Dr. Seuss thing, Chris.

CHRIS.

Can we stay focused?

DR. V.

Forgive me. Um, cell phones have been around for quite a while now. What happened in the last week to cause you so much pain?

CHRIS.

They're just everywhere. McDonald's, the gas station, the grocery store, the zoo, your office! I can't get away from them. No matter where I go, there they are—ringing! And they don't just ring… they play songs. They talk. They cry and they cock-a-doodle doo! I can't stand it. Every time I hear one, I just want to take it and shove it up someone's ass.

DR. V.

You went to the zoo?

CHRIS.

No. Why?

(She takes a moment to decide if it's worth going down this road, ultimately decides it's not.)

DR. V.

No reason.

CHRIS.

Then can we focus, please?

DR. V.

Again, forgive me. Now, you said that, uh, every time you hear a cell phone ring you want to shove it up someone's ass...that sounds pretty serious.

CHRIS.

It is serious.

DR. V.

You're 28.

CHRIS.

Yeah...so.

DR. V.

So... cell phones have literally been around for the better part of your entire life.

CHRIS.

I'm missing your point.

(They stare at each other for an uncomfortable amount of time. Eventually Chris clears his throat in annoyance. Dr. V stares at Chris a while longer. She eventually gets up to get a glass of water but thinks better of it and takes a shot of whiskey. Chris reacts to the doctor's action but does not say anything. It is evident that Dr. V is going through something, and we wonder if she is about to snap. She returns to her seat, picks up her notebook before putting it back down and staring at Chris again.)

CHRIS.

Are you okay?

DR. V.

(Checking her notes as if the last few minutes didn't happen) Forgive me, but playing songs and talking and cock-a-doodle doo-ing is not ringing.

CHRIS.

(Confused) So?

DR. V.

So, I thought only the ringing bothered you.

CHRIS.

What?

DR. V.

The ringing…?!

CHRIS.

I don't understand what you're getting at….

DR. V.

You said the phones at work, you know, in the call center, don't bother you because they don't ring—they beep, correct?

CHRIS.

Yeah, so.

DR. V.

So, songs and talking and cock-a-doodle doo-ing—which, for the record I haven't heard in years—is also not ringing.

CHRIS.

I don't understand.

DR. V.

Aw, hell. It's the fear of nickels all over again.

CHRIS.

I'm sorry, what?

DR. V.

(Writing in notebook) Nothing. Where were we?

CHRIS.

Cell phones. They're everywhere. The constant ringing....

DR. V.

Right. Is it just cell phones or do you want to shove land lines up people's asses, too?

CHRIS.

No one has land lines anymore.

DR. V.

I do. And there's also one here, in this office—that actually rings.

CHRIS.

I'm not sure what this has to do with my issue with cell phones. Can we focus, please?

DR. V.

Of course. Again, forgive me. So, tell me. How does it make you feel?

CHRIS.

Are you kidding me? I've been coming to you every week for 6 years and the best you can do is "how does it make you feel?"

DR. V.

Yes.

CHRIS.

It pisses me off.

DR. V.

So, go with it.

CHRIS.

With what?

DR. V.

Be pissed. Don't try not to be. Every single time a ringing phone pisses you off, you just be pissed.

CHRIS.

But I'm trying not to be pissed.

DR. V.

Therein lies your mistake. You're trying too hard not to be pissed when all you really need to do is be pissed.

CHRIS.

So, you're telling me to just be pissed?

DR. V.

    Yep. Be pissed. All I want you to do—is concentrate on being pissed.

CHRIS.

    But what about all the cell phones?

DR. V.

    Forget about 'em.

CHRIS.

    I can't just "forget 'em." They're the reason I get pissed in the first place.

DR. V.

    Do you have a cell phone?

CHRIS.

    Yes.

DR. V.

    Does it ever ring?

CHRIS.

    No.

DR. V.

    Never?

CHRIS.

    No. Never.

DR. V.

    No one ever calls your cell phone?

CHRIS.

   No!

DR. V.

   Why not?

CHRIS.

   I don't give out the number.

(Alex's desk phone rings. She ignores it.)

DR. V.

   So, why do you have the phone?

CHRIS.

   For emergencies.

(Alex's phone rings again; she continues to ignore it.)

DR. V.

   May I see it?

CHRIS.

   What?

DR. V.

   Your phone.

CHRIS.

   I don't have it.

(Alex's phone rings again; she checks her watch.)

DR. V.

   Where is it?

CHRIS.

At home.

(Dr. V writes in her notebook as Alex's phone rings again. She finally answers it.)

ALEX.

Thank you for calling It's All in Your Head. How may I help you?

DR. V.

But what if there's an emergency?

CHRIS.

I'll use your phone.

ALEX.

I'm sorry, but she is with a patient—

DR. V.

What if you have an emergency on your way home?

CHRIS.

I live less than a block away. Remember, I moved a few months ago to be closer to your office.

DR. V.

Yes, I know, but…never mind….

(Silence. Dr. V's phone rings; Chris jumps, suddenly affected by land lines.)

DR. V.

(Exasperated) Yes, Alex. This better be important.

ALEX.

I just thought you'd want to know that Mrs. Smith's husband is on line one. I told him you were with a patient, but he insists on speaking with you.

DR. V.

(Standing) I'm sorry Chris, but I really must take this call. The next time you get pissed, stop whatever you're doing and just be pissed. Don't think about the phones even if you believe they're the reason you're pissed. Just stop and be pissed.

CHRIS.

Exactly how is being pissed going to help me?

DR. V.

(Grabs Chris' arm to 'help' him stand) Why don't you try it for a week, and I'll see you next Thursday.

(She pushes Chris out.)

…Mr. Smith - I hope everything is alright with your wife. I was just mentioning to my assistant that we haven't heard—. … I'm sorry. I didn't know…. No, she hasn't called. Is there anything I can—. … No. Of course. I understand.

(She hangs up the phone, obviously disturbed by the conversation; looks up to see Alex standing in the doorway eating a Twizzler or filing her nails or some other random act).

ALEX.

So, did you fix her?

DR. V.

Bitch.

(Lights fade. End Scene.)

SCENE III

A week later. Alex is not at her desk. Max is in her usual position on the doctor's couch. She is wearing sweats and a stained t-shirt. Dr. V, a bit disheveled in appearance herself, is pacing in the office, repeatedly checking the time on her clock, watch and phone. Every few seconds, she checks the outer office to see if Alex has arrived.

DR. V.

Ok, Max. Tell me again, from the beginning, exactly what happened.

MAX.

I'm not paying you to spend all my time repeating myself. I already told you what happened.

DR. V.

Humor me.

MAX.

I already—

DR. V.

Last time, I promise. I just need to hear the story one more time. I mean, I must be missing something cause I know good and damn well you didn't do what the hell you just sat here and told me you did. I know I'm getting older and my hearing and comprehension aren't what they used to be. The air conditioner was blowing, and I could have been distracted by whatever that smell is you brought in here with you, but I'm still finding it hard to believe that you *(pause)*—tell me again. What did you do?

MAX.

(Deep, exasperated breath) Fine. I—

DR. V.

You punched your co-worker in the face! You punched this co-worker in the face after said co-worker attempted to restrain you. Said co-worker—

MAX.

It was Janet. I punched Janet in the face.

DR. V.ERh

Janet, who you punched in the face, was attempting to calm you because you were yelling and screaming—at the top of your lungs—and I quote, "I hate you" to the kids while they ate lunch. Why?

MAX.

I told you Janet gets on my nerves. Always trying to tell me what I should and shouldn't be doing.

DR. V.

Your personal feelings about Janet aside, I think it's safe to say that Janet, who you punched in the face, was right this time.

MAX.

I was just minding my business—

DR. V.

You were screaming at children. Why?

MAX.

Because.

DR. V.

Because why, Max.

MAX.

You told me to "embrace the hate." So, I did.

DR. V.

How does "embrace the hate" translate to "yell at children"?

MAX.

I don't know!

DR. V.

Okay. Let's back up. What were you doing before you "embraced the hate"?

MAX.

I don't know. It's all a blur…

DR. V.

Max. This is serious. You do not have the luxury of playing your little bullshit games. If you want my help—

MAX.

Your help? *(Getting up)* YOUR help? Are you fucking serious right now? YOUR HELP is the reason I'm in this situation in the first place!

DR. V.

(Sitting down) I never told you to resort to violence, Max.

MAX.

No, you just told me to embrace the hate! What the hell kind of advice is that? Embrace the fucking hate.

DR. V.

Max, all I wanted you to do was focus on your feelings. It's the only way you will ever understand what's motivating you to feel the way you do. I—

MAX.

Focusing on my feelings got me ARRESTED! What the hell

kind of therapist are you?

DR. V.

The kind that wishes she could prescribe drugs. I'm also the kind that's trying to help you.

MAX.

Whatever. Look where your help got me.

DR. V.

I'm also the kind of therapist you called to bail your ass out of jail.

MAX.

Hell, it was the least you could do.

DR. V.

Damn it, Max, if you don't want my help, why did you call me?

MAX.

Who else was I supposed to call? My mother?! Besides, it's your fault I was locked up anyway.

DR. V.

(Suddenly very nervous) Max, I never told you—

MAX.

You told me to embrace the hate! Embrace the fucking hate. When, in the history of the world, has embracing hate ever been a good idea? Hitler? Hussein? Republicans? I don't know why I listened to you in the first place? Who goes around embracing hate? Like that's a thing. *(Pacing; talking to herself more so than the doctor)* Damn, maybe I should have listened to you mama. Fucking therapy. I cannot believe I've given this fool almost two thousand dollars just for her to tell me to embrace the hate. *(Stops pacing - looks at Dr. V)* You know what I'm going to do? I'm going to print a buttload of 'Embrace the Hate' t-shirts. Embrace the hate on the front; cause this fool said so and your picture on the back. What do you think about that, doc?

DR. V.

Um, you didn't tell anyone about that, did you?

MAX.

What? The t-shirts?

DR. V.

(Panicked) No! Embrace the hate! Have you told anyone about *(whispering)*"embrace the hate"?

(Max looks at Dr. V for a long moment. Eventually, she exits the office. Dr. V, about to throw up, exits to the restroom. After, we hear various objects being thrown around and finally, the sound of glass breaking. After a few expletives, Dr. V enters shaking and rubbing injured hand, still cursing. She takes out her cell phone and dials. Alex's phone rings twice before we hear Alex's voicemail: "Hey. It's Alex. If you need me, text me.")

DR. V.

(Throwing the phone at the door to the outer office) Dammit, Alex. Answer your stupid phone!

(She goes to the restroom to get a wet towel. She lies down on the couch and puts the towel on her forehead. Alex enters silently and stands over Dr. V.)

ALEX.

(Louder than necessary) You called?

DR. V.

Jesus Alex! What the hell is wrong with you?

ALEX.

I could ask you the same question.

DR. V.

I'm fine.

ALEX.

You sure don't look it.

(She takes the towel off Dr. V's forehead and goes to the restroom.)

DR. V.

Where have you been?

ALEX.

Out. I had a couple errands to run. What the hell happened in here?

DR. V.

Nothing. It's fine.

ALEX.

So everything's fine, huh? You're "fine." The disaster in the restroom is "fine." All just fine and dandy.

DR. V.

I didn't say all that.

ALEX.

You know what I think?

DR. V.

No, Alex. I do not know what you think, and I do not want to know what you think.

ALEX.

I think Mrs. Smith got you fucked up.

DR. V.

Mrs. Smith most assuredly does not got me fucked up. Mrs. Smith is fine. I am fine.

ALEX.

Okay. Keep telling yourself that. I mean what do I know? You're the therapist who is clearly in need of some "therapy." But, hey - if you say you're fine, then you're fine.

DR. V.

Thank you.

ALEX.

All I know is ever since Mrs. Smith stopped coming, you've been spewing all this go with it, feel what you feel bullshit and now your whole practice is about to go up in flames and I'm about to be out of a job.

DR. V.

How many times have I told you to stop reading my files?

ALEX.

Thirty-two.

(Alex goes back to the outer office, slamming the door behind her. Lights fade. End Scene.)

SCENE IV

The next morning. Dr. V is in her office packing up her desk. She checks her watch, shakes her head and walks over to the door leading to the outer office. Seeing that Alex is not at work, she reaches for the desk phone to call her just as the phone rings.

DR. V.

Hello. Who? Oh yes, Mr. Smith. How are you? Um hm. Yes, of course. No, I haven't heard from her since our last session.... Mr. Smith—yes.... What? I'm sorry. What did you say? ...Well, damn. When your wife told me she longed for the father she never had, I had no idea she literally meant yours. ...Yes, I imagine it is confusing for the children. ... If you'd like me to talk to them—yes, no. Of course not. I am so sorry Mr. Smith, If there is anything I can—hello. ...Fuck.

(Dr. V. starts throwing things from the desk against the wall just as Alex enters.)

ALEX.

Whoa! Hold up! What is wrong with you? What are you doing?

DR. V.

You mean besides ruining people's lives? The fuck if I know.

(Dr. V goes back in her office and starts throwing things in the box on her desk.)

ALEX.

No, I mean what are you doing with my stuff?! You've been fucking up people's lives. I don't even understand how you still have a license.

DR. V.

(*Entering from her office*) Are you serious? Are you fucking serious? I don't have any control over what people do when they leave this office.

(*She turns and goes back in her office, alternately pacing and throwing stuff in the box. She doesn't notice Max and Chris enter the outer office. Alex motions for them to be quiet as she is enjoying Dr. V's meltdown.*)

All I can do is try my best to guide them in the right direction. Help them understand and resolve whatever the fuck they think is wrong with them. I mean, how many times can I listen to same sad sack stories about mean mommies or workaholic fathers who never came to little league games? Or the "soul mate" that turned out to be a narcissistic dipshit despite the eight hundred red flags you somehow overlooked for five years. If a grown man tells you he loves you but you still don't know where he lives after you've been dating for almost a year—RED FLAG. If your girlfriend—who you've been dating for three months—shows no interest in meeting your friends or family—including your children—I'd hold off on buying the three-carat princess cut diamond ring in a platinum setting. Dumb ass. Aaaaaaargh! If one more person comes in here and says, "I'm unhappy, but I don't know why," I will fucking lose it! If you don't know why you're unhappy, what they hell you want me to do? The sheer level of ridiculousness! I mean, if it's not the parents or the relationship bullshit, it's the "I hate my job even though I haven't updated my resume in five years" bullshit. GET. ANOTHER. FUCKING JOB! And don't even get me started on the ones that MAKE UP SHIT just to have something to do every Thursday afternoon for the rest of their shitty ass lives. GET. A FUCKING. LIFE! I mean who the hell even notices cell phones anymore?

(*Dr. V collapses on the couch and starts to laugh.*)

Shit, that felt good! I must have been holding that in for a while.

(She laughs some more. As she collects herself, she sits up and sees Alex—with Max and Chris, who have entered during her rant—standing in the doorway.)

Hey Alex!

(Max and Chris are clearly angry. Alex continues to enjoy the moment.)

Aw hell.

ALEX.

(Smiling) Max and Chris are here to see you.

DR. V.

Thank you, Alex. You're fired. Please get your shit and get out.

ALEX.

What? And miss watching these people kick your ass? *(She looks at Chris:)* Well, this person *(indicating Max)* kick your ass. I'm staying right here.

DR. V.

Nobody is kicking my ass.

MAX.

(Taking off her earrings and kicking off her shoes) Wanna bet?

DR. V

(To Max) The last thing you need is another assault charge. And we both know you ain't gonna do shit, Chris. So please, sit down. Both of you.

(Dr. V walks over to Alex, grabs her by the arm and drags her to the outer office. She hands her her purse and escorts her out the main door, locking it behind her.)

ALEX.

(Offstage) Fine. But you still have to see me at Grandma's birthday party next week! And I'm telling everything!

(Dr. V walks back into her office and sits. She crosses her arms and stares at her patients. She gets up to get her notebook out of the box. She sits back down, opens the notebook, ready to take notes.)

DR. V.

Okay. Who wants to go first?

(Max and Chris look at each other, confused.)

…Doesn't matter to me. Either one. Let's go. Time is money.

CHRIS.

Well, um. I just came to thank you for your advice last week. It really helped me.

(Max scoffs.)

DR. V.

Really?! My advice helped you? Please, tell me—tell us how my advice helped you.

CHRIS.

Okay. Well, you remember you told me to "just be pissed" when I heard a cell phone ring?

DR. V.

Yes, I remember. And the next time you heard a phone ring, you focused on being pissed, realized you really weren't pissed, and now you're cured. Congratulations!

CHRIS.

Um, No. That's not what happened, at all.

(Max laughs. She stops as Dr. V shoots her a "don't fuck with me" look.)

Actually, I thought your advice was stupid when I left, but I decided to give it a chance. I wanted to do it in a controlled environment, so I ran home and got my cell phone and turned it on. I set the ringer to the most annoying one I could stand and kept playing it over and over. I even hooked it up to my Bluetooth -

(Chris looks back and forth between Max and Dr. V, clearly proud of himself; they don't return the sentiment.)

DR. V.

So...never mind. Continue with your story.

CHRIS.

Well, after about an hour—

MAX.

Hold up, wait, and what the hell?! You sat and played a ringtone for an hour because of something she said? I'll be damned! Good to know I ain't the only one getting fucked up therapy around here. At least it didn't drain your savings and cost you your job.

DR. V.

Max, I'm gonna have to ask you to go ahead and leave.

(Dr. V gets up to escort Max out.)

MAX.

But wait, don't you want to know why I'm here?

DR. V.

No. I'm good. I don't think this is going to work out for us. It's best you find someone else.

MAX.

What? No. I need to talk to you! I lost my job; Janet is suing me, and my fiancé dumped me. We never even got around to talking about him! I need help. I know exactly why I'm unhappy. You're the sixth therapist I've seen in the last two years. Help me!

DR. V.

Hmm. No. Get somebody else to do it.

(Dr. V slams the door in Max's face and goes back into her office.)

All righty, Chris. Please! Finish telling me how my wonderful advice saved your life.

(The doctor sits back with a self-satisfied grin on her face. Chris looks at her, confused as to what is going on. He looks around the room as if looking for a hidden camera or something. Just as he's about to speak, Dr. V's cell phone rings. As she reaches for it, Chris screams and leaps off the couch. Just as he's about to pounce on her, lights go to black.)

The End.

The Jasper Project Board of Directors 2023

Wade Sellers, president
Kristin Cobb, vice president
Rebekah Rice, operations manager
Emily Moffitt, secretary
Christina Xan, treasurer
Jon Tuttle, play right series director
Al Black
Libby Campbell-Turner
Kimber Carpenter
Bert Easter
Laura Garner Hine
Len Lawson
Paul Leo
Cindi Boiter, founder and executive director

www.ingramcontent.com/pod-product-compliance
Lightning Source LLC
Chambersburg PA
CBHW041132110526
44592CB00020B/2776